A Note to Parents

DK READERS is a compelling program for beginning readers, designed in conjunction with leading literacy experts, including Dr. Linda Gambrell, Distinguished Professor of Education at Clemson University. Dr. Gambrell has served as President of the National Reading Conference, the College Reading Association, and the International Reading Association.

Beautiful illustrations and superb full-color photographs combine with engaging, easy-to-read stories to offer a fresh approach to each subject in the series. Each DK READER is guaranteed to capture a child's interest while developing his or her reading skills, general knowledge, and love of reading.

The five levels of DK READERS are aimed at different reading abilities, enabling you to choose the books that are exactly right for your child:

Pre-level 1: Learning to read
Level 1: Beginning to read
Level 2: Beginning to read alone
Level 3: Reading alone
Level 4: Proficient readers

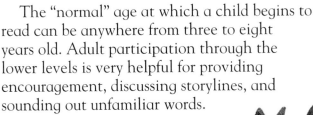

D1051626

The "normal" age at which a child begins to read can be anywhere from three to eight years old. Adult participation through the lower levels is very helpful for providing encouragement, discussing storylines, and sounding out unfamiliar words.

No matter which level you select, you can be sure that you are helping your child learn to read, then read to learn!

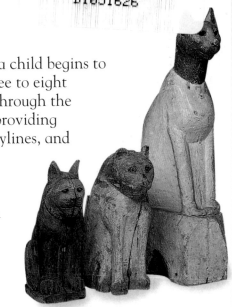

LONDON, NEW YORK, MUNICH,
MELBOURNE, AND DELHI

Project Editors Mary Atkinson
and Penny Smith
Art Editor Karen Lieberman
Senior Editor Linda Esposito
US Editor Regina Kahney
Pre-production Francesca Wardell
Picture Researchers Andy Sampson and
Kathy Lockley
Illustrator Peter Dennis

Reading Consultant
Linda B. Gambrell, Ph.D.

First American Edition, 1998
This edition, 2013
Published in the United States by DK Publishing
375 Hudson Street, New York, New York 10014
13 14 15 16 17 10 9 8 7 6 5 4 3 2 1
002—192119—July/2013

A catalog record for this book is available
from the Library of Congress.
ISBN: 978-1-4654-0940-9 (Paperback)
ISBN: 978-1-4654-0941-6 (Hardcover)

DK books are available at special discounts when purchased in bulk
for sales promotions, premiums, fund-raising, or educational use.
For details, contact:
DK Publishing Special Markets
375 Hudson Street, New York, New York 10014
SpecialSales@dk.com

Color reproduction by Colourscan, Singapore
Printed and bound in China by L Rex Printing Co., Ltd.

The publisher would like to thank the following
for their kind permission to reproduce their photographs:
c=center; t=top; b=below; l=left; r=right
AKG London Ltd: Erich Lessing 12tl; The Ancient Art and
Architecture Collection: Ronald Sheridan 3b, 17bl, 20t;
Bridgeman Art Library, London: Egyptian National Museum 17cla;
Louvre/Giraudon 7bcr; by kind permission of the Trustees of the
British Museum: 4tl, cl, 5tr, br, 6cl, 7tr, 8–9bc, 8tl, bl, 9tr, cr, 10l,
12bl, 13cr; Bruce Coleman Collection: Joe McDonald 18tl;
Colorific!: Kirsten P. Head 14cl; Mary Evans Picture Library: 20tl;
Forhistorisk Museum, Moesgard, Denmark: 4–5b; Robert Harding
Picture Library: 15tr, 16cl, 17b, tr; Walter Rawlings 17cl;
Michael Holford: 12b; Hulton Getty Collection: 14tl, 16tl;
Pelizaeus-Museum, Hildesheim, Germany: 7c, cb; Reunion des
Musées Nationaux: Louvre 11tr; Sygma: L'Illustration 19bl
All images © Dorling Kindersley Limited
For further information see: www.dkimages.com

Discover more at
www.dk.com

Contents

READERS

PROFICIENT
4
READERS

SECRETS
OF THE MUMMIES
Written by Harriet Griffey

DK Publishing

People from the past

There is something intriguing about a mummy. It is hard to believe that hundreds or even thousands of years ago it was a living person.

A mummy is the preserved body of someone who has died. The body may have been preserved naturally or deliberately as part of a religious ritual.

Naturally preserved bodies have been discovered in airless bogs. Here, the animals and bacteria that usually break down bodies cannot survive, so the body does not decay. This can also happen in hot, dry deserts and on icy mountains.

Other bodies were carefully preserved by people. The most famous mummies belong to the ancient Egyptians. But other cultures, such as the Incas of South America and the Pazyryks of Siberia, also used to preserve their dead. Some people buried their mummies with artifacts, such as bowls, statues, and beautiful jewels.

This book investigates different mummies discovered around the world. But first, let us look at how the ancient Egyptians made a mummy.

This mummy was found in a Danish bog. It is the body of a man who died more than 1,500 years ago.

Artifacts
Everyday objects were often buried with mummies.

Important doll
Figures, such as this Peruvian doll, were buried with a mummy to bring the dead person luck in the afterlife.

5

An Egyptian priest

Embalming
Chemicals, perfumes, and balms are used in this process to stop a body from decaying.

Making a mummy

For 3,000 years, the ancient Egyptian civilization flourished. The people living then had strong beliefs about gods and life after death. They thought that if a dead person's spirit could recognize its preserved body, it would live forever in the afterlife.

Rich Egyptians paid the chief priests to mummify the bodies of their loved ones. They believed that the priests could help decide a person's fate after death.

"Come quickly," a servant would plead. "My master is dead."

Right away a chief priest would send a servant to summon other priests. They would be needed to help him embalm the body—a process that stops the body from decaying.

Then the chief priest would gather his tools and set off for his workshop on the west bank of the Nile River.

Meanwhile, other servants collected the body and carried it to the workshop. There they laid it on a special table, ready for the ceremony to begin.

The chief priest put on a jackal-headed mask to represent Anubis, the Egyptian god of mummification. Then he slowly washed the body while another priest read magic spells out loud. When the body was clean enough, the embalming process began.

Tools
These tools were used in a ritual intended to enable the mummy to eat and drink in the afterlife.

This ancient Egyptian painting shows a body being washed.

Jackal mask
At embalming ceremonies, jackal-headed masks, such as this pottery one, represented Anubis, god of mummification.

After being washed, the body was left to dry.

7

The chief priest picked up his embalming knife and carefully made a long cut down the left side of the body. Then he put his hand into the cut and pulled out the liver, lungs, stomach, and guts. Each of these was stored in a canopic jar—a special container in the shape of a god.

The next part was difficult. He had to push a thin bronze hook up the dead person's nose and, bit by bit, scoop out the brain.

Incision
A cut was usually made down the left side of the body.

Embalming knife
This ceremonial knife has a sharp blade made of flint.

Hapy (HAH-pee) was a baboon god, who guarded the lungs.

The falcon god Qebehsenuef (keb-ekh-SEN-oo-ef) guarded the intestines, or guts.

The brain was thrown away because the ancient Egyptians did not understand what it was for, so they did not think it was important.

After this the body was ready to be dried. The priests heaped natron, a natural salt, over the body to draw out all the fluids. It would take 40 days for the body to dry completely.

Only then would the body be ready for the next step.

Natron
This natural salt is found by the edges of desert lakes.

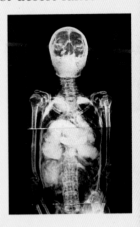

Stuffing
This X ray of a mummy shows linen stuffing replacing some of the organs.

Sons of Horus
The four gods who guarded canopic jars were the sons of Horus, god of the sky.

Imsety (im-SET-ee) was a humanlike god who guarded the liver.

The jackal-headed god Duamutef (do-ah-MOO-tef) guarded the stomach.

Magical figures
These figures lay on the body to guard the places where the organs had been removed.

Scarab beetle

Wadjet eye

Amulets
These were good luck charms. The wadjet eye was believed to keep away evil.

After 40 days, the dried body was filled with linen, sand, or sawdust to help it keep its shape. Beeswax was pushed into the nostrils, and linen was stuffed into the eye sockets. Next, oils and spices were rubbed into the skin to keep it from cracking.

Now the chief priest was ready to begin wrapping the body. He wound thin linen strips around each finger. Then he bandaged the arms and legs and the rest of the body.

Magical figures called amulets were wrapped in between the layers of cloth. At the same time, the priest brushed the bandages with resin to stick them together. Bandaging the body could take 15 days.

Finally the mummified body was placed in a coffin. If everything had gone well, the chief priest was pleased. All the dead person needed now was some magic spells.

Nest of coffins
Sometimes the coffin was put into a bigger coffin, which might then be put into an even bigger coffin, and so on.

A scribe, or writer, handed the priests a scroll. The scroll was the "Book of the Dead"—a special book containing more than 200 spells. It was placed inside the coffin.

The ancient Egyptians believed that the dead person would need to recite the spells in the book to gain protection on his or her journey to the Hall of the Two Truths.

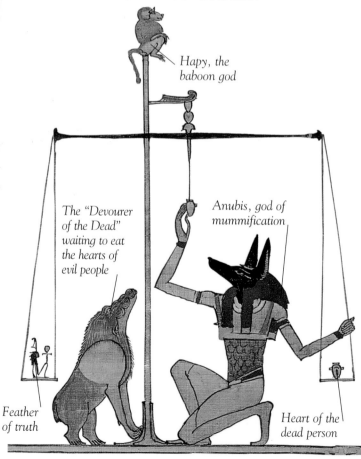

Hapy, the baboon god

The "Devourer of the Dead" waiting to eat the hearts of evil people

Anubis, god of mummification

Feather of truth

Heart of the dead person

In this judgment hall, the great god Osiris was believed to watch over a ceremony where the dead person had to deny all his or her bad deeds.

Anubis, the jackal-headed god, used scales to balance the person's heart against the "feather of truth." If the heart was not too heavy with bad deeds, the dead person was allowed to live in the afterlife.

Back in this world, the dead person's family filled a tomb with food and treasures for the mummy to use in the afterlife. Curses were often written over the coffin and the walls of the tomb, warning intruders of terrible punishments for stealing.

But over the centuries, grave robbers broke into the tombs looking for treasure. A legend grew that somewhere in the Egyptian Valley of the Kings lay a rich, untouched tomb—the tomb of the young king Tutankhamun (toot-an-KAH-mun). ❖

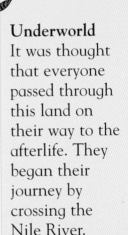

Underworld
It was thought that everyone passed through this land on their way to the afterlife. They began their journey by crossing the Nile River.

God of death
Osiris was king of the after-world, which was thought to be like Egypt but better.

13

Howard Carter
After traveling to Egypt as a young artist, Carter's interest turned to investigating ancient Egypt.

Pharaoh
The pharaohs (FAIR-ohs) were the kings of ancient Egypt. They were believed to be living gods.

The mummy's curse

"I must find the lost tomb."

Howard Carter had been saying the same thing for years. Now it was 1922, the fifth year he had spent digging through sand and rocks in Egypt's Valley of the Kings. He was searching for a tomb that no grave robbers had ever found—the tomb of Tutankhamun, the boy pharaoh.

Carter scoffed when he was warned of the curse: "Death comes on wings to he who enters the tomb of a pharaoh."

Each day, his men worked in the sweltering heat and dust. They seemed to be getting nowhere. Then one morning, as they dug in soft rubble, a shovel clanged.

When Carter arrived, he was met by an excited hush. The men had found a stone step. Another 15 steps were quickly uncovered. Could this be Tutankhamun's tomb?

Tutankhamun
This pharaoh ruled from around 1361 BC to 1352 BC. He was probably still a teenager when he died.

Valley of the Kings
To avoid grave robbers, many pharaohs chose this remote place for their tombs.

15

Carnarvon
This wealthy English lord visited Egypt for his health. His interest in tombs began as a way to pass the time.

Hieroglyphs
Each symbol in this ancient Egyptian writing stands for a word or a sound.

The staircase led to a sealed door. Carter wanted to open it, but he had to wait. Lord Carnarvon, his patron, had paid for the years of work and wanted to be present at the opening.

Today it would take only six hours to reach Egypt from Carnarvon's home in England, but at that time it took more than two weeks. When Carnarvon finally arrived, he hurried to the tomb. Nervously, he fingered the strange symbols, called hieroglyphs (HIE-row-gliffs), by the door. Then he and Carter opened the door and crept inside.

The two men pushed their way through a rock-filled corridor, which led to another sealed door. Cautiously, they made a hole in the door.

Carter was the first to look. What he saw left him speechless. Later he told people that he had seen "strange animals, statues, and gold—everywhere the glint of gold."

The room was untidily packed with priceless treasures. There were sparkling gems, animal-shaped beds, beautiful painted boxes, and a magnificent golden throne.

Nothing had been touched for 3,000 years!

Wide-eyed, the pair picked their way through the riches. Then they came to a third sealed doorway. They were desperate to know where it led, but again they had to wait. First, all these things had to be carefully sorted.

Tomb jewels
This vulture represented the goddess Nekhabet, and this scarab beetle ornament represented the sun god Khepri.

Afterlife of luxury
The ancient Egyptians filled the king's tomb with treasure, such as golden sandals and precious jewels, for him to use in the afterlife.

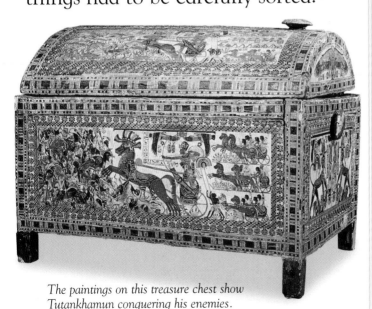

The paintings on this treasure chest show Tutankhamun conquering his enemies.

When Carter arrived home that night, his servants were wailing and shouting.

"What's wrong?" Carter demanded above the din.

"You have opened the tomb," wept a servant. "We are cursed!" He told Carter that a cobra had swallowed Carter's pet canary at the exact moment the tomb was opened. Cobras were a symbol of royalty in ancient Egypt. They were said to spit fire at a pharaoh's enemies.

Carter was not worried. The next day he began to clear the first room of the tomb.

More than a mile of cotton wadding was used to wrap up the items. Carter's team packed games, clothing, pottery, musical instruments, and statues. Most of these were sent to Cairo, Egypt's capital, by boat. The more valuable artifacts went on a train accompanied by armed guards.

Finally the men were ready to unseal the third door. Slowly and carefully, Carter started chipping away the rocks and plaster. Then he stopped. Before him was a wall of solid gold! It was the front of a huge, golden shrine. Carter was astonished. He knew this was the greatest ancient Egyptian find ever.

Cairo
Egypt's capital city grew up 1,000 years after the death of the last pharaoh.

Howard Carter (left) and his assistants carefully wrap a life-size statue.

Gold cabinet
This royal shrine filled nearly the entire third room.

Kingly coffin
The middle coffin was made of wood covered in gold with inlaid glass.

Inside the golden shrine were three more shrines. And inside the last one was a sarcophagus—a stone coffin. But that was not all. Within the sarcophagus were three more coffins, each fitting snugly inside the other. The final coffin was made of solid gold. Inside it was the mummified body of Tutankhamun.

But before anyone could investigate further, disaster struck. It began when Carter's patron, Lord Carnarvon, was bitten on the cheek by a mosquito.

He accidentally cut open the bite while shaving. The bite soon became infected, and fever set in.

A few days later Carnarvon's family raced to his bedside. He was very ill. Then, early one morning, it was all over. Lord Carnarvon died.

At the very moment of his death, all the lights in Cairo went out. They stayed out for several hours, and no one could explain why. Back at Lord Carnarvon's home in England, Susie, his dog, pricked up her ears, howled once, then dropped dead.

Other deaths followed. A French scientist who visited the tomb died after a fall. An X-ray specialist on his way to examine Tutankhamun's mummy died unexpectedly. Then a wealthy American died from a virus after visiting the tomb. Were these deaths all coincidences, or was the curse of the mummy to blame? No one knows for sure. ❖

Deadly fever
Carnarvon's razor and death certificate are reminders of how deadly a simple cut could be in the days before antibiotics were invented.

Royal mummy
Although the riches in the tomb were in good condition, Tutankhamun's mummy was badly decayed.

COLOMBIA
ECUADOR
SOUTH
AMERICA
PERU
BOLIVIA
CHILE
ARGENTINA

Inca empire
This empire covered parts of what are now Colombia, Ecuador, Peru, Bolivia, Chile, and Argentina.

Sun temples
Many temples were built in honor of Inti, god of the sun.

Inca emperor mummies

As dawn broke, drumbeats sounded through the city of Cuzco (KOOZ-koe). The people began to wake, and an excited buzz filled the air. It was the most important day of the year in the Inca empire, a civilization that covered much of South America 500 years ago.

Today was Inti Raimi (IN-tee RYE-me), a religious festival held in honor of Inti, the sun god. Every year, this festival was celebrated on June 21, midwinter's day. By showing thanks and honoring Inti, the Inca people believed that summer would come once more and their crops would grow.

Temples were built from carefully shaped blocks of stone. Sun temples were often filled with solid gold models of cornstalks, lumps of earth, and other things related to farming.

Everyone in the Inca empire gave one third of all they produced to the priests of the sun god. Many of these plants and animals were sacrificed in special ceremonies held throughout the year. Today's ceremonies were the most important of all.

Priests began to chant in time with the drumbeats. In the Holy Square, a large crowd gathered. The people were excited, but quiet and respectful. They were waiting for the Procession of the Living Dead.

Inca year
The Incas had a religious festival for each month. Inti Raimi was held in June, which is the coldest month of the year in South America.

Sun disc
The sun god was represented in many Inca temples by gold discs with human faces.

23

Llamas
The llama is related to the camel. Llamas are still used in South America for wool, meat, and transportation.

At last, the crowds spotted the white llamas that always led the procession. There were hundreds of llamas walking in lines, one after another.

Behind the llamas came a litter carrying the emperor, the Sapa Inca. Everyone in the crowd knelt down, hid their faces in their hands, and prayed. Ordinary people were not allowed to look at the Sapa Inca.

Next came litters, or stretchers, bearing the mummified bodies of the long-dead former Sapa Incas.

Each mummy was worshipped as a son of the sun god. It was thought that the living Sapa Inca received advice and help from these mummies.

Sometimes a child would sneak a look. He or she would glimpse the mummies, each draped in beautiful cloth woven from the soft wool of the vicuna, a relative of the llama.

But even a peeking child would not see the emperors' faces. They were covered with golden masks, which the priests believed would protect the emperors in the afterlife.

Litters
These beds or stretchers were used to carry the mummies in processions.

Huari mummy
The Huari people lived near Cuzco before the Incas. They too mummified their leaders.

25

Gods
Incas had great respect for their gods. They gave them offerings, such as statues, gold, animals, and sometimes even people.

Chica
This alcoholic drink was made from corn. It was stored in decorated clay jars.

The procession stopped at the Temple of the Sun, where more ceremonies began. It was a long day, full of prayer. The people thought that if they pleased the mummified Sapa Incas, they would please the sun god.

In the evening, things became a little more festive. The city's inhabitants feasted on roasted llamas served with corn cakes and potatoes. The adults drank freshly brewed chica, an alcoholic drink. There was singing and dancing until late at night. But even during the feast, the sun god was not forgotten. The very best food was put in front of the god's sons, the mummified emperors.

At the end of the day, the mummies were returned to the palaces where they had lived when they were alive. These palaces were still kept in order by specially chosen workers.

The workers fanned the air to keep flies off the mummies. They offered the mummies food and water when they felt it was needed. Most importantly, they delivered messages to the mummies and interpreted their replies.

The people believed that long-gone ancestors could give advice. It did not matter that these emperors were dead—they were still considered very powerful. ❖

Mummified bodies
For more than 4,000 years, people across South America mummified their dead.

After the Spaniards conquered the Incas in 1532, they built a church on the site of the old Temple of the Sun in Cuzco.

The Andes
This is the longest chain of mountains in the world. The Andes' snowcapped peaks run through Peru and Chile.

Look-alike
The goddess statue was made of gold and dressed in clothes similar to the girl's.

Inca ice maiden

The climbers were weary. It had taken three days to reach the top of Nevado Ampato, a high mountain in the Peruvian Andes. The paths were steep and the air was thin, making it difficult to breathe. But finally the four priests reached their destination —the top of the icy ridge.

From packs tied to the llamas, they unloaded pots, food, figurines, and a small statue of a goddess. Then they set up a small stone altar.

With the group of priests was a thirteen-year-old girl, the daughter of an important Inca family. Under a warm blanket, she wore a beautiful belted dress of rich yellow, purple, and red wool.

One of the priests led the girl to the altar. She took off the blankets, and the priest draped a finely woven cloth over her shoulders. He fastened the cloth with a silver pin.

Finally, while chanting special prayers, the chief priest placed a large feathered headdress on the girl's head.

Last resort
The Incas stored food in case of a famine. But if there was a long famine, the people appealed to the gods.

Llama herd
Statues were often used in ceremonies. This llama statue may have reminded the gods to provide grass for their herds to eat.

The unusual group had traveled to the mountain because of a severe three-year drought, or water shortage. Crops had failed and the people were starving. The priests believed that the drought occurred because the gods were angry.

After much prayer and talk, they had decided that a special sacrifice should be made to the mountain god—they must sacrifice someone who was almost perfect. That person would live forever with the gods in the afterlife. Such a sacrifice would surely please the gods and bring rain.

The girl and her family were a little frightened when she was chosen, but they also felt very honored.

Now the girl sat by a fire as the priests dug a large hole in the frozen ground. They lined the hole with sacred red earth, then placed cups, pots, and food in it for the girl to use in the afterlife.

The priests' chanting grew louder. It was time. The chief priest bent down to hand the girl a strong drink. After a few sips, she slipped into unconsciousness and died. Her body was gently wrapped in thick cloth and laid in the tomb.

When a volcano erupted 500 years later, ash fell on Nevado Ampato, melting the ice. In September 1995, scientists studying the damage found the girl's body. It had been mummified by the freezing cold. Her face had decayed, but the rest of her body was still in almost perfect condition. ❖

Mountain rescue
The two men who discovered the girl's body carried it down the mountain as fast as they could so it would not thaw and decay. It is now stored in a freezer at a university in Peru, where it is studied and preserved.

Palermo
This is the
largest city
on the Italian
island of Sicily.

Picnics
Families often
made visits to
the cemetery a
family outing
and would take
a picnic lunch!

Sicilian mummies

In the Sicilian city of Palermo, an unusual, centuries-old tradition continued right up until the 1920s.

Deep below a Catholic church was an underground cemetery, called a catacomb. It housed the mummified bodies of 6,000 people! Instead of being horrified, locals would often visit the catacomb. In the cool, dark corridors, a child would be unafraid to raise a creaking coffin lid. Inside could be the body of the child's own great-grandmother!

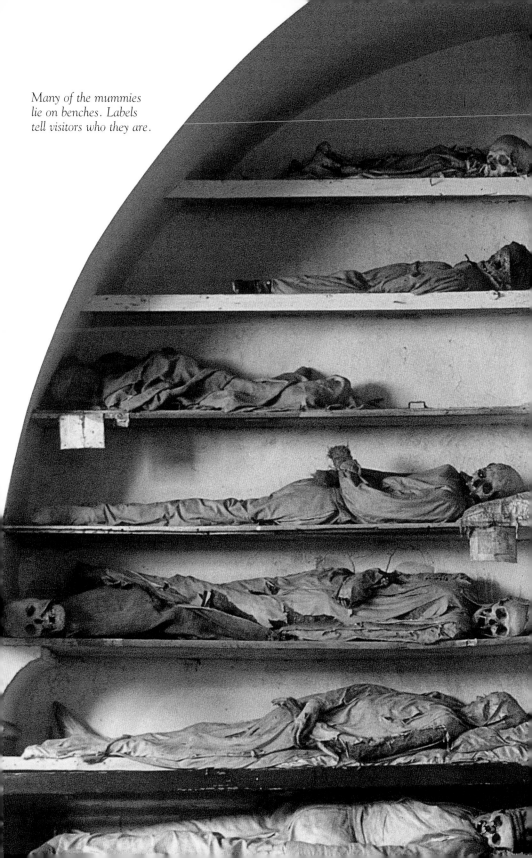

Many of the mummies
lie on benches. Labels
tell visitors who they are.

Tourist attraction
Today, the mummies of Sicily attract thousands of visitors from all over the world.

Monk
Palermo's first mummies were the bodies of highly respected monks.

The people went to pay their respects to the mummies, to tell them stories, and to ask their advice. They did not find the mummies upsetting because their families had been visiting the cemetery for more than 300 years. It was simply part of ordinary life. They believed the mummies were a link with loved and respected relatives who had died.

Occasionally the visitors would see a hooded figure moving silently among the coffins.

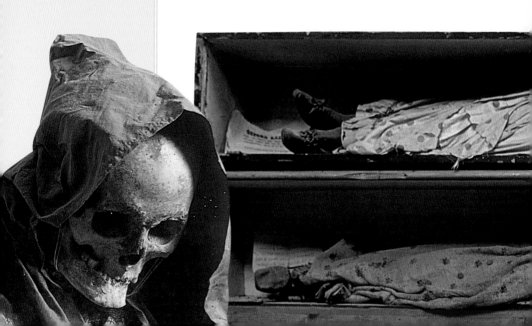

Again they were unafraid.
They knew it was just one of the
monks who looked after the catacomb.

These bearded and robed priests
lived in a monastery next to the
church. Since 1599, they had been
mummifying the bodies of respected
monks. Other people soon discovered
what was happening and began
asking for their relatives' bodies to be
mummified in return for a donation
to the church. They dressed the dead
person in his or her best clothes before
taking the body to the monastery.

Monks
The monks
who look after
the catacomb
today still wear
the brown robes
they have
worn for
hundreds
of years.

Clothing
The mummies
provide us with
information about
the styles of clothes
people wore
in the past.

35

The mummification process took over a year to complete—but how it was done was kept secret for hundreds of years!

Some of the mummies are quite gruesome to look at. The mummy of Father Silvestro da Grubbio, the oldest mummy of all, has four laughing skulls displayed around it. When Father da Grubbio died, his body was taken to a special cellar, where it lay over clay pipes for a whole year. This allowed all the body fluids to drain away.

Father da Grubbio
This monk died in 1599. The monks today give him a gentle dusting with a vacuum cleaner each year.

These pipes were used to drain the bodies.

After that, the monks laid the body in the hot Sicilian sun to dry out. Then they washed it in vinegar and, last of all, wrapped it in straw and sweet-smelling herbs. In spite of this, Father da Grubbio's mummy now looks more like a dressed skeleton.

As time went by, the monks improved their embalming process. Their new methods included soaking the body in arsenic or milk of magnesia. This left the skin far softer and gave it a more lifelike color.

The monks stopped mummifying bodies in 1920, but the mummies are still there. Today the monks take tourists around the catacomb. ❖

Soft skin
The mummies made in the 1800s still have their skin and hair today.

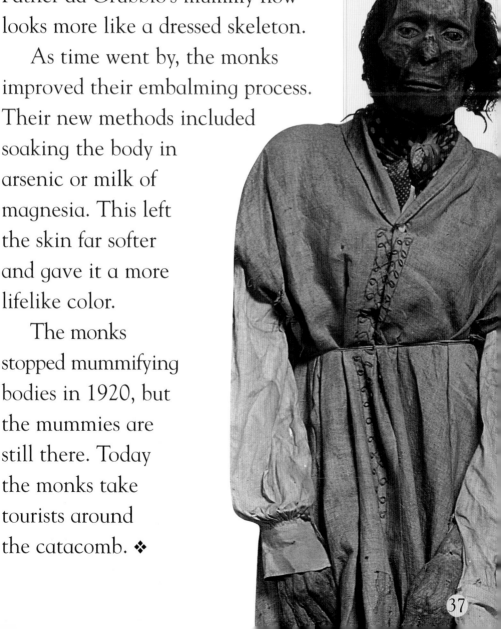

Juan Perón
Perón was the president of Argentina, the richest country in South America. Evita was his second wife.

Buenos Aires
Evita was 15 when she went to live alone in Argentina's capital city.

The mummy mystery

On July 26, 1952, Dr. Pedro Ara received the phone call he had been waiting for. "Come quickly," said an official-sounding voice, "Evita is dying. President Perón is asking for you."

Thunder crashed and rain poured as Dr. Ara hurried through the streets of Argentina's capital, Buenos Aires. After a year's illness, Evita, the president's beautiful young wife, was dying of cancer.

During her life, Evita had won the hearts of the people. She had set up hospitals and helped the poor. She had also made sure that women in Argentina were allowed to vote.

To stay popular, the president had to make sure the people never forgot his wife. He hired Dr. Ara to preserve her body. The president planned to erect a building and call it the Monument to the People. When it was built, Evita would rest there.

At 8:25 p.m., Evita died.

"This way, please." A tearful nurse led Dr. Ara down the long corridors of the presidential home to the quiet, dimly lit room where Evita lay. Immediately, the expert embalmer began his secret work.

This was to be his most important project. Evita must look as if she were sleeping peacefully, but her body must be able to last for hundreds of years.

Slowly and carefully, Dr. Ara replaced Evita's blood with glycerol, a thick liquid that would not decay. Then he placed chemicals in her coffin to kill any insects or bacteria that might attack the body. By dawn the first stage was completed.

Evita
Evita was born Maria Eva Duarte, the youngest child in a poor family. She later became a popular actress and met many important people, including Juan Perón.

Evita was a passionate speaker loved by many Argentinians.

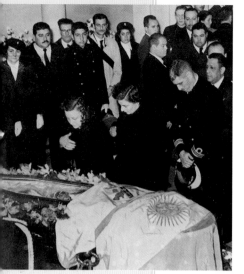

Evita's body was dressed in a white gown and placed in a glass-topped coffin. It was now ready to go on display to the public, who wanted to say farewell.

For 16 days, people lined up along the streets of Buenos Aires. More than 2,000,000 people filed past the coffin, many weeping and bending to kiss the glass lid.

But Dr. Ara began to worry. The glass case was opened twice to wipe away mist on the inside. It was not good for air to get to the body. The doctor knew he must start the next stage of the embalming process.

Sleeping beauty
People flocked to see Evita's body. Many people dressed in black or wore their best clothes as a sign of respect.

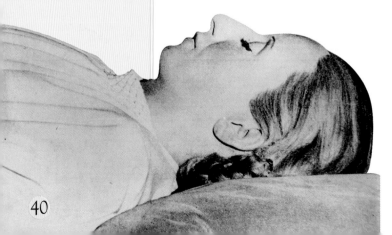

Evita looked very sick when she died. She weighed only 70 pounds (32 kg). But the embalming process made her look healthy again.

At Dr. Ara's insistence, the coffin was taken to his laboratory. There the body was repeatedly soaked in a bath of chemicals and injected with yet more preservatives. Finally, it was covered in a thin layer of clear plastic.

It took Dr. Ara a year to complete the work, but he was happy. He knew that the body would last forever.

Meanwhile, life in Argentina had become unsettled. President Perón had been overthrown by the army and forced to leave the country.

The new ruler, President Aramburu, did not want anything around that might encourage Perón's supporters. He canceled the plans for the Monument to the People. He also wanted to get rid of Evita's body, but he was not sure if the body was really hers.

A grieving nation
People had to wait hours to see Evita's body. The huge crowds stretched for 3 miles (5 km).

Floral tribute
Many people brought floral wreaths to lay near Evita's coffin. The day after she died all the flower shops in Buenos Aires were sold out.

41

President Aramburu
This army general became president of Argentina after Perón fled the country.

"It looks like a wax model," said an army officer inspecting the mummy. He checked the fingerprints. Then he had her body X-rayed. It was Evita. In fact, Dr. Ara's work was so good that even her internal organs were preserved!

President Aramburu did not want to upset the people by destroying Evita's body. It had to go—but where?

Colonel Koenig, head of Army Intelligence, offered help. Shortly afterward, in November 1955, the body disappeared.

Many stories began to circulate around Argentina about what had happened to Evita's body. Some said it had been burned, others said it was in her family's graveyard.

Then, in 1970, President Aramburu was murdered. After his death, his lawyer handed over an envelope that solved the mystery.

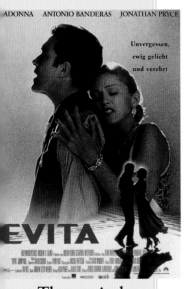

The musical
Evita's life is remembered in many books and in musical stage and film productions.

In September 1971, gravediggers at an Italian cemetery were told to open the tomb of a woman called Maria Maggi de Magistris.

Inside the tomb was a perfectly preserved body. But the body was not Maria Maggi. It was Evita Perón! The body had been secretly buried there 14 years earlier.

In 1974, Evita's body was returned to Argentina. Her long journey ended 24 years after her death when, in 1976, she was laid to rest in her family tomb. The attempt to get rid of her had failed. Today she is more famous than ever—a legend around the world. ❖

Resting place Evita's body now rests in Recoleta Cemetery in Buenos Aires. It is said to lie in a bombproof compartment.

Together again In 1974, when Juan Perón died, he was not embalmed. His closed coffin was displayed next to Evita's open one.

Evita's good works have never been forgotten.

43

Mummies today

Mummy paint
Mummies were once used to make a brown artists' pigment called *Caput Mortuum*, which means "dead head" in Latin.

Today's fascination with mummies began when the French general Napoleon Bonaparte invaded Egypt in 1798. Teams of French scholars began to study the ancient Egyptian civilization.

But much of the evidence had already been destroyed. Thousands of mummies had been burned as fuel, ground up for medicine, or simply left to decay.

The first mummies transported to the West were treated little better. Many were "unwrapped" during exhibitions, destroying vital information in the process.

Today most scientists treat the ancient dead respectfully and make the information they find widely available.

Scientists use mummies to find out what diseases people suffered from in the past. They use microscopes to look at skin, bone, and other body tissues.

Advances in technology have allowed people to take better care of ancient finds. In 1895, X rays were discovered. An X-ray picture shows scientists what is inside a mummy case. Mummies no longer need to be unwrapped to be studied.

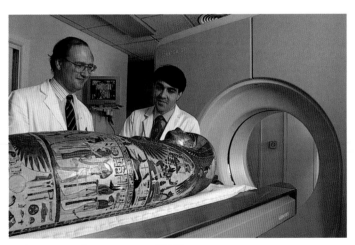
A mummy about to enter a CAT scanner

Nowadays, scientists use electronic scanners, called CAT scanners, to produce three-dimensional images of a mummy inside its bandages.

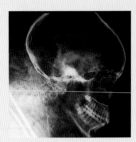

Aches and pains
This X ray of an Inca mummy shows that the brain has shrunk to a small round ball at the base of the skull.

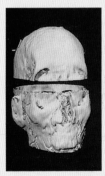

A peek inside
This CAT scan shows the skin on a mummy's face. At another setting, the machine could show the bone below the skin.

Ever present
Before he died in 1832, philosopher Jeremy Bentham arranged for his skeleton to be clothed and his head to be mummified.

While scientists study ancient mummies, funeral directors today are still preserving bodies.

Many people wish to see their dead relatives before the burial. The bodies are embalmed so that they will last a short while. They are not intended to last forever.

Evita Perón's mummy is not the only recent mummy made to last, however. As in ancient Egyptian times, today's mummies are the bodies of rich or famous people.

Thousands of tourists still line up to see the mummy of Vladimir Lenin, the Russian revolutionary leader who died in 1924.

In the US, people can pay to have their bodies frozen in liquid nitrogen. They do this in the hope that people living in the future will be able to bring them back to life.

This science is called cryogenics (kry-oe-JEN-iks). People use freezing temperatures in the same way that ice has preserved many mummies. It is already possible to bring frozen bacteria back to life. However, there is no guarantee that scientists will be able to do the same to people—yet. ❖

The mummy of Vladimir Lenin

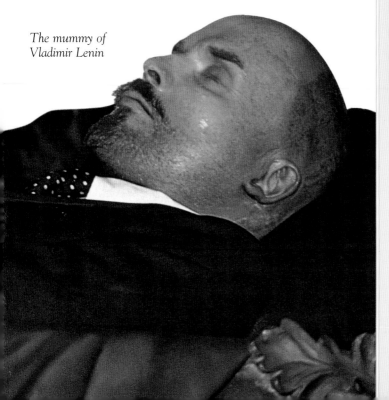

Cryogenics
When people choose to be frozen after death, their bodies are preserved in large steel containers.

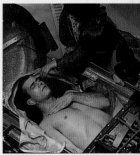

Sci-fi
Science fiction writers and moviemakers capture our imaginations with their ideas about how cryogenics might be used in the future.

47

Glossary

Afterlife
A life experienced after death. Different cultures have different beliefs about the afterlife.

Altar
A table, rock, or platform used in religious services.

Ancient Egyptians
The people living in Egypt when it was ruled by pharaohs. This was between around 3000 BC and 30 BC.

Artifact
A human-made object found at the sites of ancient homes or graves.

Bacteria
Small, one-celled organisms. Some species cause disease or break down dead matter.

CAT scanner
A computerized scanning machine that produces three-dimensional images of a person's bones and organs.

Catacomb
An underground cemetery.

Cryogenics
The process of storing bodies at very low temperatures so they cannot deacy.

Curse
A wish or spell intended to cause harm to another person.

Embalm
To use chemicals, perfumes, or ointments to preserve a body.

Hieroglyph (HIE-row-gliff)
A picture or symbol used to stand for a word or sound in ancient Egyptian writing.

Inca
A South American civilization that flourished from 1200 to 1532, when it was conquered by the Spaniards.

Litter
A bed, or stretcher, attached to poles. It is used to carry people or mummies.

Llama
A South American animal related to the camel. It is used for meat, wool, and transportation.

Monk
A man living and working in a religious community.

Mummify
The process of making a body into a mummy.

Mummy
A body that has been preserved by nature or by people.

Natron
A naturally forming salt used by the ancient Egyptians to absorb fluids.

Pharaoh (FAIR-oh)
The title given to the kings of ancient Egypt who reigned from around 3000 BC to 30 BC.

Sacrifice
To kill a person or animal in a ceremony because of a belief that it will please a god.

Shrine
A cabinet for holding a person's remains; also a place where people honor the memory of a dead person.

Tomb
A grave, monument, or small building where a dead body is stored.

Tutankhamun
(toot-an-KAH-mun)
A boy pharaoh who ruled Egypt from about 1361 BC to 1352 BC. He was probably around 16 years old when he died.

Underworld
The ancient Egyptians believed that everyone had to travel through this world beneath the earth on their journey to the afterlife.

X rays
Special rays that can pass through only the soft parts of the body. They are used to produce an image of a person's bones and internal organs.